Kundalini

A Step by Step Guide to Mastering Kundalini for Beginners in 30 minutes or Less!

Madelyn Cooper Copyright © 2015

All rights reserved. No part of this book may be reproduced in any form without permission in writing from the author. Reviewers may quote brief passages in reviews.

Disclaimer

No part of this publication may be reproduced or transmitted in any form or by any means, mechanical or electronic, including photocopying or recording, or by any information storage and retrieval system, or transmitted by email without permission in writing from the publisher.

While all attempts and efforts have been made to verify the information held within this publication, neither the author nor the publisher assumes any responsibility for errors, omissions, or opposing interpretations of the content herein.

This book is for entertainment purposes only. The views expressed are those of the author alone, and should not be taken as expert instruction or commands. The reader of this book is responsible for his or her own actions when it comes to reading the book.

Adherence to all applicable laws and regulations, including international, federal, state, and local governing professional licensing, business practices, advertising, and all other aspects of doing business in the US, Canada, or any other jurisdiction is the sole responsibility of the purchaser or reader.

Neither the author nor the publisher assumes any responsibility or liability whatsoever on the behalf of the purchaser or reader of these materials.

Any received slight of any individual or organization is purely unintentional.

Table of Contents

Introduction

Chapter 1 - Understand Kundalini

Chapter 2 - No One-Night Stands

Chapter 3 - Purification of Desires

Chapter 4 - Umm and Ohms

Chapter 5 - Rousing the Sleeping Serpent

Chapter 6 - It's Complicated

Conclusion

Bonus Chapter: Benefits of Yoga

Introduction

I want to thank you and congratulate you for downloading the book, Kundalini: A Step by Step Guide to Mastering Kundalini for Beginners in 30 minutes or Less!

This book contains proven steps and strategies for preparing yourself towards the spiritual journey of unleashing your inner Kundalini energy and mastering Kundalini awakening.

Tell me, where did you hear about kundalini? Did you stumble upon it on some flyer? Perhaps hear it from your neighbor? Did you think you need to go to India or approach some spiritual guru in order to master it?

Worry not! You can start this mystic mission by yourself at your very own home. You do not need to spend hundreds of dollars in paying a spiritual master for something that you can easily learn in this book.

If you take the time to read this book fully and apply the information held within this book will help you understand the role of Kundalini in achieving a better and higher state of consciousness, understand that it is not simply done through chanting and groaning your way through a whole hour of session. Kundalini is a delicate and mystical spiritual path that must be undertaken with faith.

This book will also help you awaken the sleeping serpent within you and reach mystic enlightenment as it isequipped with steps that will guide you in triggering your very own Kundalini phenomenon. The instructions provided for the Kundalini awakening will only take less than 30 minutes.

And this book has more to offer as it also discusses the importance of commitment, meditation and purification in your quest of mastering Kundalini.

Thanks again for downloading this book, I hope you enjoy it!

Chapter 1: Understand Kundalini

Kundalini is not a new mainstream Indian concept. It is not your latest recreational activity introduced in order to give bored individuals something novel to do. Nor is it a new method to lose weight like what others perceive the purpose of yoga is. The history of Kundalini is one filled with mysticism and spirituality. Others consider it to be the way to achieve communion with God or even attain the status of a god. It is a big stride towards spiritual evolution.

Kundalini is described as the spiritual energy dwelling within one's body that must be raised and awakened for you to achieve purification of bodily systems and reach a new state of consciousness.It is the Eastern terminology given to the energy which lies dormant and shown symbolically like a coiled snake wrapped three and a half times at the base of the spine(Kumar & Dempsey, 2002). It exists in everyone's body and lies latent until one is ready for its release or one purposely triggers it. Also known as the libidinal and unconscious force, Kundalini energy lies coiled at the base of the spine in a triangular bone called the sancrum like a sleeping serpent waiting to be awakened. It is one of the components of one's spiritual or "subtle" body along with the chakras or your psychic centers; nadis, the energy channels; bindu, which refers to the drops of essence; and prana, one's subtle energy.

Awakening Kundalini leads to enlightenment and involves the energy moving up from the base of the spine to the top of the head. The manifestation of this progress from its initial location is felt as cool breeze across the palms of your hands or the soles of your feet. However, in the case when the movement of the energy was not properly done and there is an imbalance, this breeze will seem warm across the specified areas. Do you feel a tingle or an electric current running along your spine? Then you must be feeling the movement of the Kundalini, as well. The energy passes through different chakra points which correspond to different levels of awakening and spiritual experience. Reaching the top of the head – the crown – leads to a significant and profound mystical experience. This explains why it's not a one time, big time deal. Quitting after raising Kundalini once is not the proper way to do it. On your first endeavor, you might just activate a lower level chakra point and experience a less significant spiritual experience. Moreover, enlightenment is a gradual and staggered affair. Kundalini must be raised many times before it can fully grow. A single Kundalini experience may occur for at least 5 minutes and at most 30 minutes. This duration may lengthen by training and higher development. It also depends on the energy resources of a person. If his energy is depleted, the experience implicated in Kundalini awakening may not be long.

Arousal through spiritual exercises and even spontaneous circumstances brings out a higher level of one's self. Mystical enlightenment and illumination can be achieved. We have the potential to become better than what we are now. Mastering of Kundalini would aid us in developing a different spiritual version of ourselves without the risk of our personalities being lost. If you fear that your friends will no longer recognize you after mastering Kundalini, don't fret. The traits and characteristics that made you who you are will not be buried under the new state of consciousness that you will embrace.

When you achieve enlightenment through Kundalini arousal, you will perceive the world differently. This might sound cliché but your life will change as the Kundalini energy within you will remove the veil that's covering your eyes from seeing the world. Like water, you will undergo a purification process that will eradicate the resistance and impurities blocking you from experiencing pure love, and trust, among others.

You will experience a different and more comprehensive understanding of the world and reality. You do not need to take in tablets or shoot powders up your nose anymore in order to achieve ecstasy because spiritual enlightenment would help you achieve that feeling.

Activating the Kundalini circuits is a form of transformation. Imagine yourself as larvae. It's not something ideal, is it? But once you trigger the bodily changes through Kundalini, you can unleash a new circuit that would make you turn into a butterfly. The body begins to reorganize itself after raising Kundalini and it will adapt a new state of being.

Even after a person reverts to his normal self, his consciousness and knowledge returning to its original state as well, after a Kundalini awakening, one's spiritual abilities will remain heightened and enhanced.

There are various ways as to how you can awaken your Kundalini. Gurus and spiritual masters can help as well as meditations, breathing exercises, and mantra chanting. It has been reported though that Kundalini can be spontaneously stimulated after a psychological or physical trauma. However, it is emphasized that awakenings through spiritual exercises are better compared to spontaneous ones. When it is by accident (e.g. trauma, childbirth, near-death experiences), the symptoms resemble those experienced in a true Kundalini awakening but are rather unpleasant and damaging.

There are two main approaches in awakening your Kundalini. On one hand, we have the passive approach wherein you surrender yourself to the ministrations and guidance of a spiritual master or guru. A master who has previously experienced the Kundalini phenomenon is responsible for arousing one's own.

On the other hand, we have the active approach. This book will teach you to take initiative in awakening your own energy. This method would incorporate concentration, breathing, and visualization exercises.

The first thing that you have to do before the inner serpent within you can be stirred to rise is preparation. You must first equip your mind and body with the right knowledge and state of being before you endeavor to open your spiritual channels. And knowing aboutKundalini is a very important step. Time and time again, we hear the saying, "Knowledge is power". Obviously, knowing what one is doing goes a long way in accomplishing it. If you want to try motocross racing, you don't just grab a bike from the nearest garage, turn the engine on and zoom your way into oblivion or at the very least, to the hospital. Without preparation, jumping straight into the fire is risky and dangerous. This is why a person who desires to try to awaken his Kundalini must be taught and educated in this subject matter. At times, people want spiritual development to happen with a snap of their fingers, desperate to reach the acclaimed mystical illumination. But they fail to realize that the risk level of acquiring the negative consequences is proportional to the quality of their preparation.

You must have faith in what awakening the Kundalini will achieve. A cynic who tries to open his energy channels just for the fun of it would not likely succeed in doing so. His belief system must be established first.

In arousing Kundalini, you should also know that chakra centers play very vital roles. There are 6 chakra centers associated in the Kundalini process. These centers will amass energy and once it reaches its peak, energy would be released in an upward flow towards the top of the body, triggering the chakra centers above. A Kundalini phenomenon which is fully raised is called the internal snake phenomenon. When this happens, one feels like as if a literal snake pushes its way up between your anus and genitals. It then travels in a spiral up through the body, pushing your organs and internal body parts out of the way along the process.

For one to raise a full Kundalini phenomenon, one must gather a lot of energy at the base chakra center. Through practice, you can become better in accumulating energy in your centers and once the energy mass reaches critical points, it would be released. One of the physical manifestations of this explosion of energy is a tingle or electrical spike along the spine.

Chapter 2: No One-Night Stands

The next step in your preparation is committing yourself to the journey. Doing Kundalini should not arise from a desire to conform to what other people are doing or because you think it's cool. You also shouldn't do it just so you could have something to post as a Facebook status or tweet. Egoistic tendencies must be eradicated when you want to master Kundalini.

Additionally, awakening the sleeping energy within you requires a commitment in your part to be faithful to the spiritual path. Kundalini isn't just about achieving ecstasy. It's about developing a spiritual consciousness that will transform you as a person.

It also takes commitment to go through the exercises that can arouse your Kundalini energy. You can't just say you've had enough after your first attempt. Quitters are losers. Look at it this way. You enter into a relationship. Without commitment, you'd probably end up breaking it off with your partner after the first few weeks because it has become tiresome and full of hassle. Without commitment, you'd just leave your partner in bed after the first orgasm! It's not a relationship then, but a one-night stand. There is no one-night stand in the case of awakening your Kundalini energy. The spiritual path doesn't encourage the participation of those whose hearts are not into the task.

It is a transformational process that you can't afford to just stop according to your whims. You also need to stand by whatever consequences you will gain as Kundalini has been implicated to have long-term, transformational effects that may be strong enough to change the structure of our DNA, causing changes to even the cells (Lim, ND). In other words, this is serious stuff. There is no joke hidden that you can read between the lines.

Full awakening would probably take a longer time that you have anticipated if you do not take this earnestly. Actually, the length of the process depends on every individual. If you have the necessary mindset and have prepared well, mastering it would not make you break a lot of sweat.

So, ask yourself why you are doing this. Do you believe in Kundalini, in the first place? Did you just do this because you happened to hear your colleague at work speak this foreign word?

If you do believe in it, invest your thoughts into the proper execution of this process and be exacting in the observance of the steps. Don't do anything half-heartedly because it's no better than not doing this at all. Any hesitation or doubt to the experience may lead to complications to your psyche. It may even be permanently damaged because of the mental perspective that you don on while you take this course.

Also, do not allow other people to influence what you believe in. Others might find the whole concept of the Kundalini energy to be preposterous and associate it with another Indian mumbo-jumbo. As long as you have faith, nothing and no other opinion matters. Fact is: you are doing this for yourself and not for them.

Chapter 3: Purification of Desires

Do not let earthly desires occupy your every thought. You want more dollars in your bank account? You want to be more beautiful or successful or popular? That's fine but don't let it fill up every nook and cranny of your mind 24 hours a day. In awakening your Kundalini, you should endeavor to free your minds of impurities such as wants and needs in order to prepare yourself to the energy that will soon be coursing through your body.

In your Kundalini sessions, try not to let thoughts of what you want to eat for dinner interrupt your meditation. The goal of arousing the sleeping energy within you is the achievement of enlightenment and mulling over how fried chicken is so delicious will not help you achieve your endgame.

Furthermore, in order to prepare one's body for a spiritual awakening, detoxifying it from impurities is a must. Our energy flows through our bodies which serve as vehicles. Imagine your spirit energy as the driver and your body as the car. Everything that you do to your car will have consequences on the probability of reaching your destination. The food that you eat which enters your body and the secretions from the glands which leaves it will affect your chakras.

One must consume clean fuel sources – that is, a diet rich in nutrients makes up for a healthy life force. Processed foods will introduce toxins into the vehicle and would only lead to its deterioration. Fruits and vegetables will aid in easier digestion and would not fatigue your body so much. Consumption of junk foods is also discouraged since they definitely do not bring in nutrients into your body and can just create organ complications. Take note that what you eat is the fuel of your car. Imagine that instead of gasoline which is the proper source of energy needed to run your car, you feed it with orange juice or muddy water. OJ can't make your vehicle run and not only that.It would most likely destroy some parts of your car.

Likewise, your body needs the proper sources of energy. Not everything that is edible is appropriate.

Additionally, drinking plenty of water is not only beneficial for your physical body but also for your spiritual one. Avoid drinking alcoholic beverages. Most importantly and obviously, do not partake in any alcoholic drink as you are about to engage in a Kundalini session because it will mess with your energy centers and with the clarity of your thoughts.

One should also abstain from drugs. Not only do these substances create negative effects on the physical body, they also lead to the deterioration of your psychological and mental capacities. Getting high is neither a form of higher consciousness nor does it help you achieve that state.

Tobacco is another no-go. You already know that smoking has detrimental effects on the lungs and on the brain. A major element in awakening your Kundalini is breathing and without your lungs to facilitate that action, you are doomed. Plus, smoking takes in dangerous toxins into your body, the very thing that we wish to avoid.

Ridding the body of toxins can also be done though body secretions. Run maintenance tasks on your vehicle through engaging in physical activities such as exercise. Sweat out the toxins from your body. But always remember not to overdo as any excess may lead to your body collapsing from the overworking. Moreover, don't shock your body into doing things it has never underwent before. If it's your first time to exercise, do not go all out and implement a training program containing an hour of cardio exercises, 2 hours on the treadmill, 100 crunches, and so on. You must gradually introduce your body to these activities and implement them slowly in order for the mind and body to adapt.

You can choose to run or bike for one hour a day to help the body be freed of the toxins. Put another resolution in your list which is to test and try your limits. If you can only bike for an hour, add another ten minutes the next time you do so. Use your mental power to push through your limitations. This will exercise your willpower and increase your concentration which you will need in awakening your Kundalini energy.

From time to time, you can have a full body massage to release the tension from your body. It would help in the better circulation of blood throughout your body and in opening up your chakra centers.

Other hormonal secretions must also leave the body before you undertake Kundalini awakening. If you are sexually tense and need a release, do it and don't rob yourself of the opportunity. Restricting oneself would just prove to be detrimental since it would distract your mind from concentrating on the proper exercises when it's time. Instead of relaxing and focusing on your breathing, you might end up fidgety and uncomfortable after the sexual repression.

Chapter 4: Umm and Ohms

In order to prepare and build your mind and body for Kundalini awakening, you must practice yoga and meditation. Meditating will familiarize you with the concentration and mental stability needed in spiritual exercises. You can start with simple meditation exercises such as emptying your mind and feeling your breathing. Another meditation exercise involves imagining a bright star whose light you will take in into your body.

If you immediately jump into doing the steps for Kundalini exercises, you might find it hard to focus without any prior experience.At first, you might find your thoughts careening around your mind like kids overdosed with candies. Any sound you will perceive can break your concentration and distract you. The first time trying to keep these thoughts in check would prove to be disastrous and exhausting. But, continuous engagement in trying to rein them in would make you more capable in the future. Meditation exercises will allow you to take control of your thoughts and their directions.

Do the meditation exercises as often as you can in order to train your mind. Your first ever Kundalini event may not prove as successful as intended because your mind haven't been trained enough to concentrate and focus.

Furthermore, practicing yoga will improve the connection between your mind and body. It refers to the joining together of the different consciousness in your body and mind. Yoga will allow you to realize your limitations and break through them. As you might have noticed in yoga exercises, there is an emphasis on how mental power can control the physical self. Through willpower and focus, you are able to execute physical postures and stances that you thought to be beyond your capabilities.

Sometimes, it's thinking of the words *no, can't,* and *impossible* that causes one's failures in any task. When your yoga instructor tells you to do a full lotus, negative thinking about the flexibility of your legs would make you not attempt to follow through. But if you train your mind to think *yes,* it's no longer mission impossible. Try to shift your perspective into a more positive one.

There are various yoga exercises that you can participate in as preparation for your Kundalini awakening which includes Hatha Yoga, Raja Yoga, and Bhakti Yoga. The steps that you can learn from the aforementioned forms of yoga can also be combined and used during your proper awakening. You can take elements from these yoga forms and prepare your mind and body through their combination.

Chapter 5: Rousing the Sleeping Serpent

Find a place or a spot you are comfortable in. It is important that you are at a place where your focus won't be easily broken or disrupted. Somewhere in nature is ideal. You can park yourself beside a pond, for example, or near a waterfall. However, if you do not have access to this kind of setting or don't have the time to reach one, you can choose a room that you can arrange to become more proper and suitable. Adjust the room's lighting and temperature. During the session, cellphones and other electronic devices must be turned off since they serve as distractions.

In lieu of the real deal, you can also decide to listen to some music of nature or just have silence as your company. Sounds of nature like that of flowing water and birds chirping could be ideal to stimulate the energy within you.

It is also important to start a session with the proper state of mind. If you are sick or troubled, it wouldn't be advised to follow through with the process. Pick a time wherein you don't have responsibilities and obligations to fulfill and answer to. Make sure that during the session, you would not be interrupted by your boss calling or a friend asking for a companion to the salon.

Prior to the session, you can also lower the stress level of your body by getting a full body massage in order to release the tension from your muscles.

Now, let's talk about the steps that you will need to master Kundalini awakening.

The first thing that you have to do is sit comfortably. Determine a position where you will not cramp your limbs or hurt any body part. Wear comfortable clothes, as well. Choose those which will not constrict your movements and your breathing. It would not do well to start awakening your Kundalini only to faint because your shirt is so tight that you can't breathe.

Inhale. Exhale. Breathe deeply. Regulate your breathing as rhythm is very important since it facilitates concentration.

Empty your mind of your daily worries. Stop thinking of the future and don't dwell in the past. Don't reminisce about your ex-loves and what you did at work earlier. Don't ponder on the trip that you have wanted to take for so many years now. Focus on the present and focus on your breathing.

As you breathe deeply, feel the air passing through your nose. Feel the oxygen passing through your nostrils and expanding your lungs with life.Inhale. Exhale. Feel the sensation of tranquility and peace embracing you. Feel the comfort embracing you as you continue breathing deeply. Relax your muscles. Feel the way your limbs are doing away with the tension. Feel your arms going loose. Be at ease with how your body feels.

Now, begin to focus your breathing at the base of your spine, the base chakra center. Feel your breathing. Fill your base chakra center with a pleasant sensation. Remember a time when you experienced a deep, pleasant sensation and fill the base of your spine with this feeling. Feel it opening and being filled with a pleasant feeling. Feel it opening and becoming filled with energy.

Continue to breathe deeply through your nose as you inhale and exhale. Allow the air to move into you, bringing life as it moves down into your lungs. Focus your breathing into your chest, at your heart. Feel it contracting as it pumps blood into your veins. Recall a memory when you felt a pleasant sensation at this center and bring that happy feeling into your heart. Think of a time when you were in love, when you felt elation and intense happiness. Feel your heart energizing, filling up with that wonderful sensation. Feel your heart and chest expanding with as they become full of the joyful sensation.

Bring your focus now in the middle of your neck. Breathe deeply. Inhale and exhale and concentrate on this area. Fill this chakra center with a pleasant sensation. Fill it up. Open it wider and wider and pour energy into it as you breathe deeply.

Continue to breathe deeply through your nose. Now concentrate on the next chakra center, on your third eye which is located on your forehead. Begin to breathe into this energy center. Feel the air energizing you and energizing this center. Feel your chakra energizing and think of a time when you felt a wonderful sensation in that area, something to make this energy center feel full. What about a beautiful memory. Bring the feeling from that moment into this moment. Open up this center and feel the clarity of thought, the absence of worries and clutters. Fill this center with positive sensation.

Bring your awareness now to your crown chakra located at the top of your head. Feel the energy moving through your body as you breathe deeply. Breathe and send the life the air gives you to your crown chakra. Feel it open and expand, becoming wider.

Bring your spine into a straight position. But do not forget to be comfortable. Relax your posture but straighten your spine. Feel your spine moving as it straightens. Feel every movement of your joints, vertebrae, as your spine becomes completely straight. Now, feel your energy center at the base of your spine. Breathe deeply into this energy center and feel it becoming open and active, widening and opening. Breathe deep.

Then breathe into the next energy center. Feel your chest expanding as the base of your spine is opening. Breathe deeply into both energy centers.

Breathe into the middle of your neck. Open this center and fill it with energy, with pleasant sensation. Breathe. Energize the three energy centers. Feel it brimming with sensation. Feel the wonderful sensation coursing throughout your body.

Focus now on your forehead. Make it active by pulling all the energy from the other centers into this center. Allow the energy to travel. Breathe deeply; let the energy flow from your nostrils into your lungs, into your spine and back up again into your chest, into your throat, and into your forehead.

Maintain your focus and continue to breathe deeply. Let the energy travel from the other energy centers into the energy center on your forehead. Fill it up with energy. Maintain the beautiful sensation of connection. Recall beautiful feelings and pour them into your energy centers.

Now, you are energizing every chakra center in your body. Feel the beautiful sensation all throughout your body. Maintain the pleasant sensations in these areas. Bring the energy from the base of the spine all the way up to your crown chakra.

Maintain the sense of depth and the sensations. Feel the connectedness within you. Continue to breathe deeply into these areas. When you are ready, begin to come back into your waking life with all these energy running through your body. Maintain your breathing. Open your eyes slowly and gradually come back to your wakeful existence.

Now, the energy is streaming through your body and the experience would last depending on how well you have executed the steps. The physical symptoms of the awakening may last up to 30 minutes and with repetition, you can lengthen this.

Alas! After only 30 minutes or even less, you have mastered Kundalini awakening. The degree to which your Kundalini may have arisen depends on your state of mind and your observance to the steps.

The movement of Kundalini, as it moves through the chakra centers, is felt in various physical manifestations. During the process, your body might tremble and an electric current might run along your spine as the energy in your chakra centers explode. There have been reports that during the flow of Kundalini upwards, sound like that of a flowing waterfall, tinkling ornaments, birds chirping, may be internally perceived and heard. Your mouth may also fill with saliva. The symptoms may also differ across situations. In one session, you may feel your head getting heady and feel bright lights behind your eyes but in another session may hear sounds and feel sexual tension.

The experience will not be identical on every individual. Don't worry if what you go through differs from what you've heard since it is affected by your specific situation.

Remember to relax your focus. Don't force it. As you focus the energy up from the chakra centers in the lower parts of your body up towards your crown chakra center, you allow the energy to move on its own.

Moreover, don't think that the steps are too ridiculous to perform. You might wonder why and how you could focus your breathing into energy centers where air doesn't normally flow into. But it's actually effective to think of your breathing as a way of moving your energy around. When you focus your breathing in a specific chakra center, the energy flows to that area.

Chapter 6: It's Complicated

Now that you are aware of the steps you need to take to master Kundalini, take the first steps towards your spiritual journey. However, you must heed some warnings regarding this mystical adventure. In every endeavor, there are always risks when they're not done with prior knowledge and preparation.

In the case of Kundalini, there is such a thing as premature awakening. Not everyone is fit to have their energy awakened. Let's take physical exercise as an example. If you are like the majority of people who have hated PE classes when they were required during high school and college, you probably forsake any kind of task that puts demands you to strenuously move. But let's say that a circumstance has come up and it expects you to exercise through jumping over ropes 100 times in a minute. Can you do it? Maybe you have arthritis or maybe your body is not just strong enough for this kind of physical torture. The answer, then, is *No*. So, should you push it? Again, *No!* If you will, you would probably end up face first on the floor. This logic also applies to Kundalini awakening. A balanced and strong mind coupled with a balanced personality and body is needed as raising Kundalini demands a great deal of energy and willpower.

When either the mind or body is unprepared, it can be overwhelmed and this would lead to complications. The experience felt when this is the case is called *Kundalini syndrome*.

One's nervous system could be overloaded. In this situation, you'll end up in a ward, dressed in white and screaming "I'm not crazy" to the staff, because of a psychotic break. An unprepared person could also suffer disassociation from reality as a result of hasty proceedings. You might end up believing you're in Hogwarts even when you are obviously not.To add, severe anxiety wherein you will worry over the simplest of things could render you incapable of performing daily activities. Additionally, there were reports of disorientations and physical complications like sexual dysfunctions and gastrointestinal disorders (Kundalini Complications, ND). Insomnia and involuntary movements could also result from premature awakening.

These complications from premature arousal is explained to be consequences of one's Kundalini energy encountering barriers as it progresses from the base of your spine to the top of your head. These barriers could be in the form of toxins that one didn't eradicate from the body or even thoughts that proved to be disruptive to the flow of energy.

Going through the awakening while your mental state is so troubled that no meditation can empty it is a no-no. Aggression, violence, and other negative dispositions could also be detrimental. Negative emotions will always be discouraged because in an effort that involves the spirit, malevolent thoughts and feelings are not welcome.

So remember to not take the immediate plunge towards Kundalini arousal. Remember the tips – understand Kundalini, purify your body of the toxins, and meditate. They are recommended for a valid reason which is to ready your body and mind.

Conclusion

Thank you again for downloading this book!

I hope this book was able to help you to become more familiar with what Kundalini is. You might just have heard of Kundalini from your neighbor and thought it as another Indian fad. But at this point, you know that it is more than that as it is a long-term goal that requires dedication, hard work, and faith. You are now equipped with the knowledge regarding this delicate spiritual journey. I hope this book was also able to teach you what you need to do before you engage in rousing your inner serpent and guide you with the steps in doing so. Take note of the importance of adequate knowledge, proper meditation, and a balanced mind and body.

The next step is to take heed of the tips and warnings that come with triggering your spiritual energy. You are now armed with guiding words into taking that step towards a higher state of consciousness and enlightenment.

Remember that this spiritual path must not be taken out of boredom or simple curiosity. It takes commitment and discipline in order to stick to the principles of Kundalini.

Finally, if you enjoyed this book, please take the time to share your thoughts and post a review on Amazon. It'd be greatly appreciated!

Thank you and good luck!

Bonus Chapter: Benefits of Yoga

There are many benefits to yoga. Some types of yoga, such as Kundalini yoga, can constitute good exercise that is healthy and low impact that nearly anyone can do. Yoga can also benefit you in numerous other ways, both in the body and mind. These benefits have been well documented by osteopathic doctors from all over the nation and the world.

Yoga is not just a physical activity. It's a relaxation technique. This allows yoga to offer many more benefits than other types of exercise. In fact, yoga could be the answer for many people who cannot or do not want to do heavy physical activity.

Benefits of Yoga as an Exercise

Many people do not want to consider yoga a form of exercise. However, exercise does not need to be strenuous to be effective. Yoga offers the same types of benefits as other exercise. It offers increased flexibility and improved muscle tone. It helps with a balanced metabolism and can even help you lose weight.

Yoga also offers protection from injury, improved athletic performance and promotes cardio health. Even though most yoga is not physically active, performing yoga does in fact increase your heart rate, allowing you to have the benefits of cardio exercise without the strenuous activity.

Benefits of Yoga in Chronic Pain and Illness

Yoga has been known to lessen chronic pain in a number of instances. It can alleviate lower back pain through the combination of stretching and relaxation. It can also help ease pressure and pain from arthritis. Even chronic headaches can be eased through yoga.

Yoga also helps unhealthy people lower their risk for serious chronic illness. Yoga lowers blood pressure, lowering risk for heart disease. The way it balances your metabolism can help diabetics manage their blood sugar, as well as decrease your chances of developing diabetes if you have other risk factors.

Because yoga is relaxing it is a great way to combat insomnia. People with high anxiety and high stress have also reported benefits of yoga, claiming that the relaxation combined with physical activity helps to calm them and make them more at ease. Insomnia, anxiety and stress have been proven to have a serious effect on health, including causing migraines, ulcers and increasing risks for heart disease. Yoga combats all of these with ease.

Benefits of Yoga on the Mind

The relaxation and meditative state achieved by yoga has incredible benefits for the mind. The deep breathing and stretching of the limbs puts the mind at ease. Even the most stressed, most upset person can be instantly calmed by a session of yoga. The more at ease the mind, the healthier the body. This is why yoga is the ideal exercise. It benefits mind and body together, and recognizes that the two should be in harmony for perfect health.

Working Yoga Into Your Daily Routine

For the most benefit, you should work yoga into your daily routine. Many people consider exercising just one time a day, and potentially not every day. However, yoga is different. You can benefit from yoga every day, and multiple times of day. However, the types of poses you do should vary depending on what time of day you are doing them.

It is generally recommended to practice yoga in two sessions, one in the morning and one in early evening. In the morning you will do invigorating poses designed to start your day right with abundant energy and clarity. In the early evening you will want to do poses that are relaxing and calming, giving you a new perspective and preparing you for rest.

You may also want to do yoga in the afternoon. Afternoon yoga poses should include those mostly for meditative purposes, or for a change of perspective. Afternoon yoga sessions are mostly for a break from the daily routine, and a way to relax and bring yourself back into focus to finish your day.

Made in the USA
Middletown, DE
04 November 2015